United States Presidents

Franklin Pierce

Anne Welsbacher

ABDO Publishing Company

visit us at
www.abdopub.com

Published by ABDO Publishing Company 4940 Viking Drive, Edina, Minnesota 55435. Copyright © 2001 by Abdo Consulting Group, Inc. International copyrights reserved in all countries. No part of this book may be reproduced in any form without written permission from the publisher.

Printed in the United States.

Photo credits: Corbis

Contributing editors: Tamara L. Britton and Christine Phillips
Book design and graphics: Patrick Laurel

Library of Congress Cataloging-in-Publication Data

Welsbacher, Anne, 1955-
      Franklin Pierce / Anne Welsbacher.
          p.   cm. -- (United States presidents)
      Includes index.
      Summary: A biography of the fourteenth president, who served during a period of increasing bitterness between the North and the South.
      ISBN 1-57765-247-9
      1. Pierce, Franklin, 1804-1869--Juvenile literature. 2. Presidents--United States--Biography--Juvenile literature. [1. Pierce, Franklin, 1804-1869. 2. Presidents.] I. Title. II. Series: United States presidents (Edina, Minn.)
      E432.W43   2000
      973.6'6'092--dc21
      [B]   98-7933
                                                                                   CIP
                                                                                   AC

Contents

Franklin Pierce 4

Early Life 8

Law and Politics 10

Representative Pierce 12

The Youngest Senator 14

The Making of the Fourteenth
    United States President 16

General Pierce 18

President Pierce 20

The Seven "Hats" of the U.S. President 24

The Three Branches of the U.S. Government... 25

Final Years 26

Fast Facts 28

Glossary 30

Internet Sites 31

Index...32

Franklin Pierce

*F*ranklin Pierce became the fourteenth president in 1853. During his term, arguments over slavery grew into an event called Bleeding Kansas. Homes burned and people died.

While president, Pierce bought land from Mexico. He also opened trade between the U.S. and Japan.

Pierce was born in New Hampshire. He went to college in Maine. Then he became a **lawyer**. He was a New Hampshire **legislator**. Later he was elected to the U.S. **House of Representatives** and the U.S. **Senate**.

Pierce married Jane Means Appleton. They had three children, but all three died young.

Pierce fought in the **Mexican War**. He rose from colonel to **brigadier general**.

While Franklin Pierce was president, he could not stop the fighting over slavery. But he helped the U.S. buy new land and improved trade with other countries.

President Franklin Pierce

Franklin Pierce (1804-1869)
Fourteenth President

BORN: November 23, 1804

PLACE OF BIRTH: Hillsborough, New Hampshire

ANCESTRY: English

FATHER: Benjamin Pierce (1757-1839)

MOTHER: Anna Kendrick Pierce (1768-1838)

WIFE: Jane Means Appleton (1806-1863)

CHILDREN: Three boys

EDUCATION: Bowdoin College

RELIGION: Episcopalian

OCCUPATION: Lawyer, soldier

MILITARY SERVICE: Brigadier general in U.S. Army

POLITICAL PARTY: Democrat

OFFICES HELD:	Member and Speaker of New Hampshire legislature, New Hampshire district attorney, U.S. House of Representatives, U.S. Senate
AGE AT INAUGURATION:	48
YEARS SERVED:	1853-1857
VICE PRESIDENT:	William R. King
DIED:	October 8, 1869, Concord, New Hampshire, age 64
CAUSE OF DEATH:	Dropsy

Detail Area

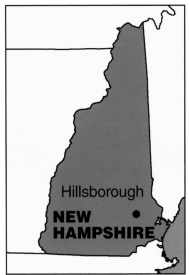

Hillsborough

NEW HAMPSHIRE

Birthplace of Franklin Pierce

Early Life

*F*ranklin Pierce was born on November 23, 1804, near Hillsborough, New Hampshire. His parents were Benjamin and Anna Pierce. He was the youngest of seven children.

Benjamin Pierce owned a farm and a tavern. He was state **legislator** and governor. He also fought in the **American Revolution**.

Franklin loved to listen to his father's war stories. He also liked to fish and trap animals.

Franklin's two older brothers fought in the **War of 1812**. Franklin often waited at the post office for their letters about the battles. He wanted to be a soldier, too.

But Franklin had to go to school. First he went to a small school called Hillsborough Center. When he was 12, he went to the Hancock Academy.

Franklin was a good student. He stayed in during recess to help other students with their work.

Pierce's childhood home in Hillsborough, New Hampshire

Law and Politics

*I*n 1820, Pierce went to Bowdoin College in Brunswick, Maine. He enjoyed spending time with other students.

At first, Pierce was a lazy student. He had the worst grade in his class.

Then he decided to get a better grade. He studied all day. He slept four hours at night. Soon, he was one of the best students in his class.

Pierce was elected captain of the Bowdoin Cadets, a marching and drill club. He took part in **political debates**. He graduated in 1824. Then he went home to Hillsborough.

In 1825, Pierce decided to study law. First he studied under Levi Woodbury in Portsmouth. Then he went to law school in Northampton, Massachusetts. There he studied under Edmund Parker.

Pierce passed the **bar exam** in 1827. He returned to Hillsborough to open his own law firm.

In 1829, Pierce was elected to the New Hampshire state **legislature**. He was on the **Committee** of the Whole. He kept order during many fierce debates.

In 1831, Pierce became **Speaker** of the **legislature**. He was only 26 years old. He helped pass bills to open new banks and aid the poor.

In 1832, Pierce was elected to the U.S. **House of Representatives**. But he became very sick with **cholera**. When he felt better, he left for Washington, D.C.

Bowdoin College

Representative Pierce

*I*n the **House of Representatives**, Pierce did not make many speeches. Instead, he worked hard on **committees**.

Pierce served on the Judiciary Committee. He renewed patents. He gave people financial aid. He also helped people learn about bills and laws.

In 1834, Pierce supported a bill to close the Bank of the United States. He thought the bank only helped rich people. The bank closed in 1836.

Pierce also voted against a bill to build railroads and canals in the U.S. He thought this would take away each state's independence.

Then Pierce met Jane Means Appleton. She lived in Amherst, New Hampshire. They were married on November 19, 1834. Then they moved to Washington.

During this time, the country was arguing over slavery. Some states wanted slavery and some did not.

In 1835, Pierce supported the gag rule. It said no one could talk about slavery in **Congress**. He thought this would help stop the arguing in Congress.

Pierce also spoke against the United States Military Academy at West Point. It was a school to train soldiers. Pierce thought some of the students might not go into the military. He felt this would waste government money.

In 1836, Pierce voted to recognize Texas as independent. Americans **debated** over whether or not Texas would have slavery.

On February 2, Pierce's first son, Franklin, Jr., was born. But he died three days later. The Pierces spent the summer in Hillsborough. That fall, Pierce was elected to the U.S. **Senate**.

Jane Pierce

The Youngest Senator

*P*ierce was the youngest **senator** elected in 1836. He worked on the Pension **Committee**. It gave **veterans** money. In 1837, Pierce supported a list of rules written by Senator

John Calhoun. They said that each state could decide whether to have slavery. This way, states could not control each other.

In 1838, Jane got sick. She wanted to move back to New Hampshire. So Pierce bought a house in Concord. Then he opened a new law firm there.

That same year, their son Frank Robert was born. Then their son Benjamin was born in 1841.

John Calhoun

The Pierces' home in Concord

In 1842, Pierce left the **Senate**. He moved back to Concord to be with his family.

Pierce worked at his law firm. He argued for farmers whose land was being taken to construct railroads. He felt this was unfair. In 1843, Frank Robert died.

In 1844, Pierce worked on James K. Polk's presidential campaign. Polk won the election. Later, Polk appointed Pierce New Hamphire's **district attorney**.

President James K. Polk

The Making of the Fourteenth United States President

1804
Born November 23 in New Hampshire

1820
Enters Bowdoin College

1824
Graduates from college

1825
Attends law school

1827
Passes bar exam

1834
Marries Jane Appleton November 19

1836
Son Franklin Jr. born; elected to U.S. Senate

1838
Son Frank Robert born; family leaves Washington for Concord

1841
Son Benjamin born

1842
Leaves Senate; joins family in Concord

1847
Appointed brigadier general in army

1848
Mexican War ends

1852
Elected president

1853
Son Benjamin dies

PRESIDENTIAL

Franklin Pierce

"With the Union my best and dearest earthly hopes are entwined. Without it what are we individually or collectively? What becomes of the noblest field ever opened for the advancement of our race in religion, in government, in the arts, and in all that dignifies and adorns mankind?"

1829
Elected to New Hampshire state legislature

1831
Becomes Speaker of the legislature

1832
Elected to U.S. House of Representatives

Historic Events
during Pierce's Presidency

★ British inventor George Cayley builds the first glider

★ Florence Nightingale pioneers modern nursing in the Crimean War

★ Famous painter Vincent Van Gogh born

1843
Son Frank Robert dies

1844
Polk elected president; appoints Pierce New Hampshire district attorney

1846
Mexican War begins

1854
Gadsden Purchase; trade opens with Japan; Ostend Manifesto; Kansas-Nebraska Act

1857
Travels to Europe

1863
Wife Jane dies

1869
Dies October 8

YEARS

General Pierce

*P*resident Polk wanted to make Texas part of the U.S. But Mexico wanted to control Texas. So in 1846, the **Mexican War** began.

Polk asked Pierce to be U.S. **attorney general**. But Pierce said no. He wanted to fight in the war.

Brigadier General Pierce

In 1847, he was appointed colonel of **infantry** for the army. He helped raise money for the soldiers. He spoke about the war at town meetings.

Then Polk made Pierce **brigadier general**. Soon, Pierce joined General Winfield Scott in Mexico. He led 2500 soldiers towards Mexico City.

On the way, Mexican soldiers shot at Pierce and his men. The guns scared Pierce's horse. The horse threw Pierce. His knee was hurt badly.

In Mexico City, the Mexicans

surrendered to the American soldiers. The war ended in 1848. Pierce went home to Concord.

In 1852, the **Democrats** held their **convention** to pick a candidate for president. Some wanted a president who would allow slavery. Others wanted a president who would not.

There were many candidates. But the Democrats could not decide who to **nominate**.

Then they nominated Pierce. He believed each state should have the right to decide if it should have slavery. Many of the Democrats agreed to vote for him.

Pierce ran against **Whig** party candidate Winfield Scott. Pierce won the election.

General Winfield Scott

President Pierce

*I*n 1853, Pierce and his family took a train to Concord. The train fell off the tracks and rolled down a steep hill. Pierce and his wife were not hurt. But their son Benjamin was killed.

Pierce went to Washington. He was still mourning the death of Benjamin. Jane was so sad that she became weak and sick. That same year, Vice President William King died.

In 1854, Pierce sent railroad company president James Gadsden to Mexico to buy land west of Texas. Pierce wanted this land to build a railroad across the U.S.

In the Gadsden Purchase, the U.S. paid Mexico $10 million for 26,670 square miles (76,845 sq km) of land. This land is now southern New Mexico and Arizona.

In 1818, the U.S. and Canada agreed to share fishing rights off Canada's coasts. But in the 1850s, Canada began to seize American fishing boats.

In 1854, Pierce made a **treaty** with Canada. The U.S. could fish off Canadian coasts. And Canada could trade cheaply with the U.S.

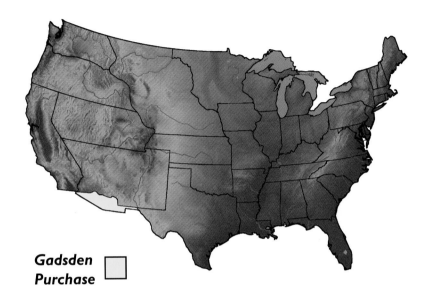

Gadsden Purchase ☐

    Then Pierce sent Commodore Matthew C. Perry to Japan. Perry convinced the Japanese to open two ports to the U.S. The U.S. and Japan could trade for the first time.

    That same year, Pierce wanted to acquire Cuba from Spain. He wanted to add new land to the U.S. His cabinet members wrote the Ostend Manifesto. It stated that the U.S. should seize Cuba.

Many Americans thought acquiring Cuba was a good idea. But others were afraid Cuba would become a slave state. So the U.S. did not acquire Cuba.

In the 1850s, people began to settle in Kansas and Nebraska. In 1854, Pierce passed the Kansas-Nebraska Act. It said the new states could decide whether or not to have slavery. It ended the **Compromise** of 1820 that had banned slavery in this area.

James Buchanan

Pierce sent Andrew Reeder to be Kansas's governor. He set up a **proslavery** government and **constitution** in Lecompton.

But in 1855, **abolitionists** established their own government in Topeka. And they wrote their own constitution.

Soon people were fighting over which government was right. The fighting became bitter. Many people died. This time is called Bleeding Kansas.

Pierce supported the proslavery government. He believed it was created at a legal **constitutional convention**. The fighting slowed, but it did not stop. The slavery issue was dividing the country.

Many people were angry with Pierce. They blamed him for the fighting in Kansas. Many people did not like his plan to seize Cuba, either.

Pierce was not **nominated** for president in 1856. The **Democrats** chose James Buchanan to run instead.

The United States during Pierce's presidency

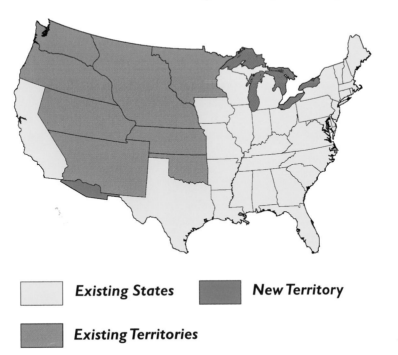

Existing States

New Territory

Existing Territories

The Seven "Hats" of the U.S. President

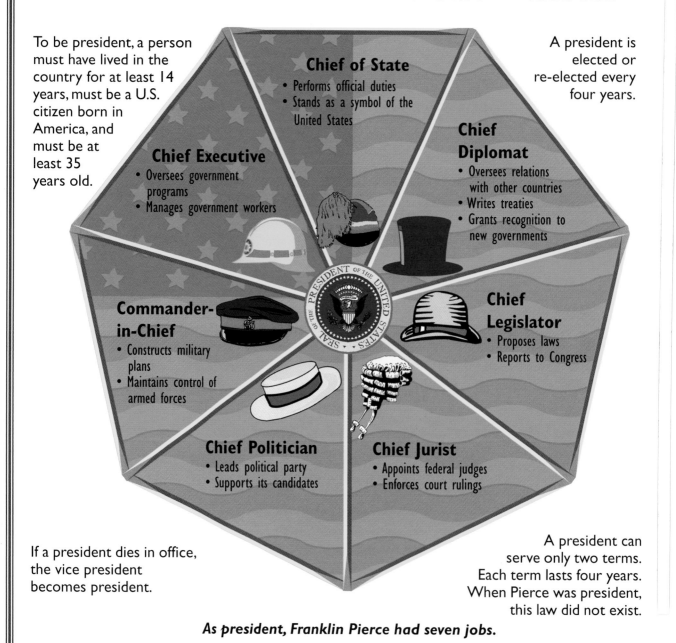

To be president, a person must have lived in the country for at least 14 years, must be a U.S. citizen born in America, and must be at least 35 years old.

A president is elected or re-elected every four years.

Chief of State
- Performs official duties
- Stands as a symbol of the United States

Chief Executive
- Oversees government programs
- Manages government workers

Chief Diplomat
- Oversees relations with other countries
- Writes treaties
- Grants recognition to new governments

Commander-in-Chief
- Constructs military plans
- Maintains control of armed forces

Chief Legislator
- Proposes laws
- Reports to Congress

Chief Politician
- Leads political party
- Supports its candidates

Chief Jurist
- Appoints federal judges
- Enforces court rulings

If a president dies in office, the vice president becomes president.

A president can serve only two terms. Each term lasts four years. When Pierce was president, this law did not exist.

As president, Franklin Pierce had seven jobs.

The Three Branches of the U.S. Government

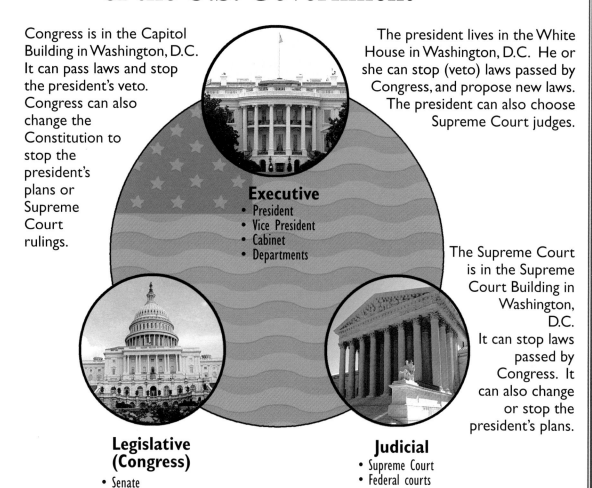

Congress is in the Capitol Building in Washington, D.C. It can pass laws and stop the president's veto. Congress can also change the Constitution to stop the president's plans or Supreme Court rulings.

The president lives in the White House in Washington, D.C. He or she can stop (veto) laws passed by Congress, and propose new laws. The president can also choose Supreme Court judges.

Executive
- President
- Vice President
- Cabinet
- Departments

The Supreme Court is in the Supreme Court Building in Washington, D.C. It can stop laws passed by Congress. It can also change or stop the president's plans.

Legislative (Congress)
- Senate
- House of Representatives

Judicial
- Supreme Court
- Federal courts

The U.S. Constitution formed three government branches. Each branch has power over the others. So no single group or person can control the country. The Constitution calls this "separation of powers."

Final Years

*F*ranklin and Jane Pierce left Washington, D.C. in March 1857. Jane was still sick and sad. The Pierces traveled to Europe to make her better.

In 1859, they returned to New Hampshire. They bought a new house outside of Concord.

Pierce gave **political** speeches. He tried to **unite** the country on the slavery issue. He thought people should follow the **Constitution**.

Jane Pierce died in 1863. Pierce died of **dropsy** on October 8, 1869.

By making the Gadsden Purchase, Franklin Pierce added new land to the U.S. And he increased trade with Japan and Canada. During his presidency, many people fought over slavery. But Pierce worked hard to keep the country together.

A rare photograph of Franklin Pierce

Fast Facts

- Pierce was the first president to give his **inauguration** speech from memory.

- Pierce's father, Benjamin Pierce, fought with George Washington during the **American Revolution**.

- The college Pierce went to was very strict. Students were not allowed to see any shows, play cards, go fishing, sing, or even clap their hands!

- While he was in college, Pierce made friends with a student named Nathaniel Hawthorne. Hawthorne wrote Pierce's **biography**. Later, he became an important American writer.

- Pierce is an **ancestor** of Barbara Bush and her son, Texas governor George W. Bush.

Barbara Bush and her son, George W. Bush

Glossary

abolitionist - someone who is against slavery.

American Revolution - 1775-1783. A war between Great Britain and its colonies in America. The Americans won their independence and created the United States.

ancestor - a person from past generations to whom one is directly related.

attorney general - the chief law officer of a national or state government.

bar exam - the test a person must pass to become a lawyer.

biography - the story of a person's life.

brigadier general - a commissioned officer in the U.S. Army, Air Force, or Marines, ranking above a colonel and below a major general.

cholera - a disease of the intestines that includes severe vomiting and diarrhea.

committee - a group of people chosen to do a special task.

compromise - settling a disagreement by having both sides give up some of what they want.

Congress - the lawmaking body of the U.S. It is made up of the Senate and the House of Representatives.

Constitution - the document containing the supreme law and plan of government of the United States. Each state also has a constitution.

convention - a large meeting set up for a special purpose.

debate - to discuss a question or a topic.

Democrat - a political party. When Pierce was president, they supported farmers and landowners.

district attorney - a lawyer who represents the government in a certain district, such as a county.

dropsy - an unnatural amount of watery fluid in the body.

House of Representatives - a group of people elected by citizens to represent them. It meets in Washington, D.C. and makes laws for the nation.

inauguration - when a person is sworn into office.

infantry - the soldiers trained and organized to fight on foot.

lawyer - a person who knows the law and acts for another person in a court of law.

legislature - the lawmaking group of a state or country. A legislator is a member of this group.

Mexican War - the war fought between the U.S. and Mexico between 1846 and 1848.

nominate - to name a candidate for office.

politics - the process of making laws and running a government.

proslavery - believing that slavery is right.

Senate - a governing or lawmaking assembly.

Speaker - the leader of the majority party who runs legislative sessions.

surrender - to give up.

treaty - a formal agreement between two countries.

unite - to join together.

veteran - a person who has served in the armed forces.

War of 1812 - the war between the U.S. and Great Britain between 1812 and 1815.

Whig - a political party that was very strong in the early 1800s, but ended in the 1850s. They supported laws that helped business.

Internet Sites

The Presidents of the United States of America
http://www.whitehouse.gov/WH/glimpse/presidents.html
This site is from the White House.

PBS American Presidents Series
http://www.americanpresidents.org
This site has links and information on Franklin Pierce's life.

Historic Hillsborough
http://www.conknet.com/~hillsboro/historic/historic.html/html
This site has information on Pierce's childhood home and town.

These sites are subject to change. Go to your favorite search engine and type in United States Presidents for more sites.

Index

A

American Revolution 8, 28
attorney general, U.S. 18

B

Bank of the United States
        12
birth 4, 8
Bleeding Kansas 4, 22, 23
Buchanan, James 23

C

Calhoun, John 14
children 4, 13, 14, 15, 20
Compromise of 1820 22
Congress, U.S. 12
Cuba acquisition 21, 22,
        23

D

death 26
Democratic party 19, 23
district attorney, New
        Hampshire 15

E

education 4, 8, 10

G

Gadsden, James 20
Gadsden Purchase 20, 26
gag rule 12

H

health 11, 18, 26
hobbies 8, 10
House of Representatives,
        U.S. 4, 11, 12

K

Kansas-Nebraska Act 22
King, William 20

L

lawyer 4, 10, 14, 15

M

Mexican War 4, 18, 19
military service 4, 18, 19

O

Ostend Manifesto 21

P

parents 8
Perry, Matthew C. 21

Pierce, Benjamin (son) 14,
        20

Pierce, Frank Robert (son)
        14, 15
Pierce, Franklin, Jr. (son)
        13
Pierce, Jane (wife) 4, 12,
        13, 14, 20, 26
Polk, James K. 15, 18
president 4, 19, 20, 21, 22,
        23

R

Reeder, Andrew 22

S

Scott, Winfield 18, 19
Senate, U.S. 4, 13, 14, 15
siblings 8
slavery 4, 12, 14, 19, 22,
        23, 26
state legislature 4, 10, 11

T

Texas annexation 13, 18

W

War of 1812 8
Whig party 19